Needle Felting

For Beginners

Lori Allen Rea

First published in the United States of America by Lori Rea

ISBN: 978-1-7343141-1-3

www.naturecrafty.com

Contents

Needle Felting for Beginners was first published as an ebook in 2017 and has over 7,000 downloads to date.

This new 2020 edition, in both print and ebook, has been completely redesigned with new projects and photography to better reflect the advances in techniques and technology.

This book is specifically designed to teach the complete beginner in a sequential manner, with easy but inspiring, step-by-step project-lessons. Each project builds on the next, adding skills bit by bit, without overwhelming the newbie.

Comprehensive explanations on wool, needles and tools plus an extensive and up-to-date resource section, gives you the confidence to buy the right supplies without wasting valuable time or money.

The **next book** in this series, *Needle Felting - A Complete Course,* is designed to take your needle felting skills to the next level with projects that include armature building and more intricate pieces.

Wool Chart for projects

Specific amounts/weights needed are given in the individual project instructions. Batt is usually sold in 1 or 2 oz. bundles. Natural color, or core batt is best to buy in larger amounts.

Colors names are different for each vendor, use this chart as a guide when choosing colors.

Batt

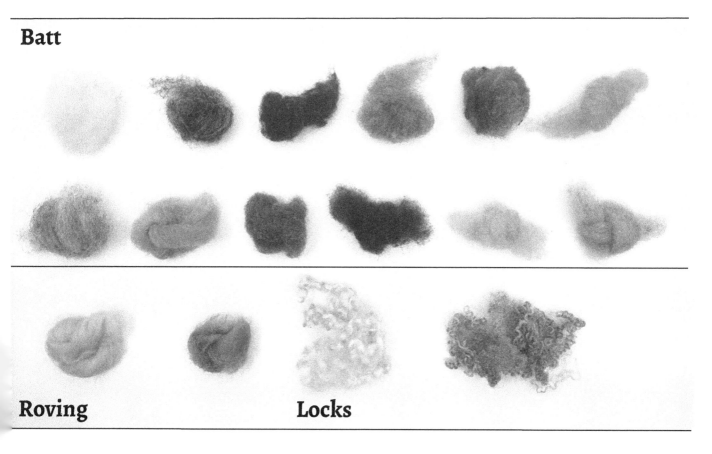

Roving   **Locks**

Introduction

Welcome to the adventurous new fiber art of needle felting! This concise, instructional book will guide you through the basic fundamentals of using a needle and wool to create fantastic needle felted sculptures.

The first part of the book covers important foundational topics such as: wool, needles and basic techniques. The project section includes pieces that start at the beginner level and move on to more challenging work. All the projects are designed as sequential lessons, to build your skills incrementally. When you have worked through this book, you will be ready for more advanced pieces and the second book in the series, **Needle Felting - A Complete Course**.

When I first started felting in 2010, I found it hard to locate basic information that was presented to the beginner in a step-by-step system that made sense. I tried to piece information together from websites and videos. Most available books were more about promoting the specific style of the author than it was about teaching skills to the beginner. I saw a need for a guide that a newbie could use to get started quickly and confidently. After several years of obsessive felting on my own, I decide to write a tutorial book with clear pictures and instructions, edited down to the key elements and that would give the beginner confidence, move them forward quickly and help them to get started designing their own projects.

What Is Needle Felting

Needle felting is a craft that uses wool and special felting needles to create wool sculptures, which can be both 3-dimensional (sculpture) or 2-dimensional (flat). To needle felt something, a notched needle is repeatedly stabbed into the wool. The wool fibers have scales that tangle together and lock when the wool is stabbed with the notched felting needle. The wool condenses and shrinks as it is repeatedly stabbed, therefore giving the wool the ability to be shaped and create sculptures.

History of Needle Felting

Needle felting, as an art, was born in the 1980's when Eleanor Stanwood took industrial felting needles and applied them to making handmade wool sculptures. Needle felting grew slowly for a few decades until it began to take off in the 2000's as more information became widely available on the internet. Although still considered in its infancy, there has been astounding growth in needle felting as evidenced by the many fabulous artists that showcase their pieces on social media.

Basic Techniques

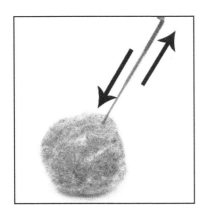

How to use a needle
Needles must be poked into the fiber and removed from the fiber at the same angle. If you twist or bend your needle during this process in any way, the needle will break. You can put a needle in at any angle, but it must be removed at the same angle it went in. Using a needle in needle felting is called "stabbing" or "needling".

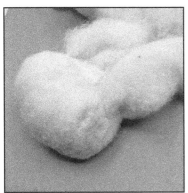

How to make a core shape
To make a tight inner core, start by rolling your wool very tightly, and felt down with each turn, or roll. Doing this cuts down felting time by 70%. Your goal is to remove the air or "loft" from between the layers as efficiently as possible. *Stabbing as you roll,* is the quickest way to accomplish this.

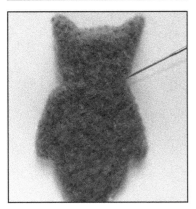

Making a piece firm
A needle felted sculpture has 3 levels of firmness:
* Soft - springy, squishy, easy to pull apart
* Medium - Semi-firm, not easily pulled apart
* Firm - Very slight to no indentation when pressed.
Firmness is obtained by doubling your stabbing time after the piece reaches the medium stage.

Attaching pieces
Attaching two pieces can be achieved in several ways.
* Layer one piece on top of another and stab through both pieces until they can't be pulled apart.
* Attach a piece by adding a layer or piece of wool between the two elements you wish to put together.

How to make your piece smooth

Smooth finishes depend on several factors.
Batt, roving and top can be made into a smooth finish.
Using a #40 or #42 needle helps give a smooth finish as these needles leave smaller holes. You can shave your piece after it's done or iron it. Occasionally you can wet-felt a project to smooth it as well.

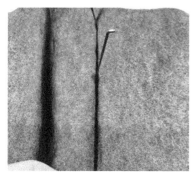

How to make a thin line

The best type of wool for thin lines is combed top. Pull off a small amount of top and twist the strands together. Pin the top of the strand where you need it to be and then it will stay in place as you felt the twist down onto your piece.

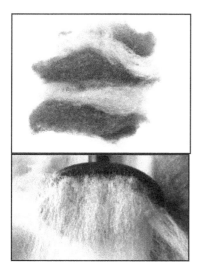

How to blend colors

To hand blend, layer one color on top of another for two or three layers. Then, pull that entire piece in half, placing the bottom over the top, rip and repeat over and over until the wool is blended.
Dog brushes or hand carders also work well for blending. Don't try and mix different types of processed wool, for example: batt does not blend well with top or locks.

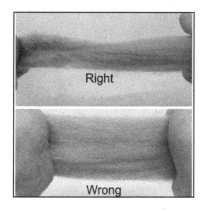

How to divide wool

When dividing batt, simply rip off the amount you need. For roving or top, grasp in-between a length of rope, hands placed about 10" apart, and pull. If your hands are too close together the top will not rip apart. Scissors are not recommended as they leave a hard edge on the wool that is hard to felt into projects.

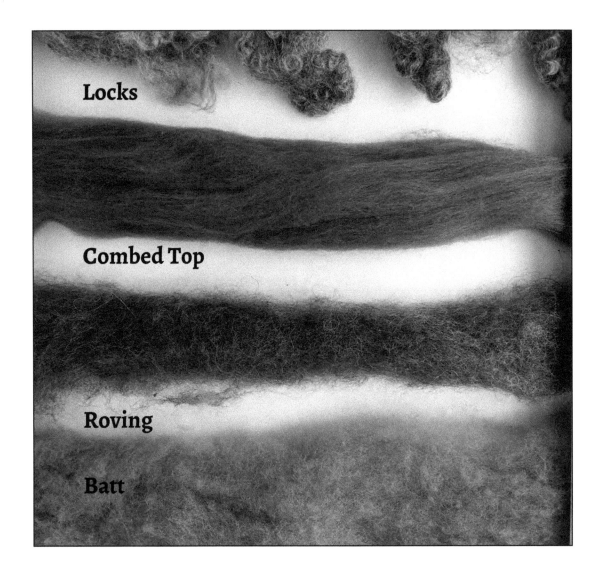

Locks

Combed Top

Roving

Batt

Breeds

Choosing a breed of sheep's wool, if you are buying locally, will depend much on your geographic area. The fibers of certain breeds are more suited to needle felting than others. For your first order of felting wool, I strongly recommend that you stick with established needle felting store recommendations. Specialty felting stores often sell a wool product that is a mixture of breeds to bring about the best outcome for needle felters.

Below are a list of only a very few breeds available for felters.

Merino - fine, soft and often used as a top coat
Corriedale - A medium fine wool, firm and smooth
Blue Faced Leicester - A long, fine wool, soft and beautiful locks
Shetland - Fine wool with crimp, readily available
Romney - A medium to coarse wool, felts well and a favorite of many

Wool

Wool can come from a variety of animals. For needle felters, sheeps wool is the most common choice and the gold standard for felting. It is extremely important to have an understanding of wool: processing type, breed and quality. The wool needs of needle felters can be very different from the other fiber arts. There are over 200 breeds of sheep in the world and depending on where you live, some breed types will be more readily available than others. For the beginning needle felter it is best to purchase wool from the established felting stores as they stock wool specifically for needle felting (see shopping resources).

Wool Products

Batt is a carded wool and is sometimes known as core wool as it it used for the base, or core of the project. It is usually less expensive (natural color) and therefore economical to use for the bulk of your project. The fibers in batt go in all different directions and it is coarse and fuzzy looking. *Batt felts up firmly and quickly* and is wonderful for 3-D as well as 2-D projects.

Combed Top, or "top" for short, is created by brushing the fiber in the same direction. It is smooth and has a sheen to it. Top works well for the top coat of any piece. It is sold in a huge variety of colors and is often used to finish a piece. It is soft and also used in wet felting. *Do not use this for core felting, it felts slowly.*

Roving is sold in rope form but it is very similar to batt in that the fibers are flowing in different directions. People often confuse the roving and top because they are both sold in rope form but roving is much more coarse. *Roving is great for core work and for wrapping armatures.*

Locks are the curly or crimped looking part of the fleece that has been washed but not processed. It is used for visual interest in wall hangings and things like beards or doll hair.

> **Think of a cake when you are choosing wool products for your project.**

Batt is the core (the cake middle)
Top is the icing (top coat)
Locks are the decorations

Needles

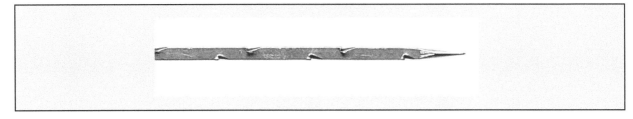

Needles are where the magic of needle felting starts. When you stab into wool with a notched felting needle, the notches on the needle grab and tangle the wool and mat it all together, condensing it and giving the artist the ability to make a sculpture. There are two factors to consider when choosing a needle: type and gauge.

Needle Gauges

Felting needles are sized by their diameter or gauge, meaning size. The lower the gauge, the better it is for fast felting. It is a stronger needle. The higher the gauge the better it is for finer work, it is thin and it leaves less visible holes.

#32 - #36 - These gauges are good for felting quickly, they can handle core work. They leave a larger hole and are not recomended for top coats.

> **#38** - This is the one needle gauge that can do almost anything and is the best choice for a beginner. You can do both core and top coat work with this multi purpose gauge.

#40 - #42 - These needles are for fine work like adding details and thin lines to pieces. They leave very few visible holes. Use for finishing and 2-D work.

Needle Types

Triangle blade - A triangle needle has 3 sides with 2 notches per side. This is the most common choice and is good for all-purpose felting.

Star Blade - This needle has 4 sides with 2 notches per side. It has more power behind it to felt things up quickly. Good all purpose needle.

Spiral blade - A spiral, or twisted needle is the same as a triangle needle only the notches corkscrew up the blade and they leave less noticeable marks. They are good for fine work.

Reverse (inverted) blades - This needle pulls fibers OUT of the sculpture instead of pushing them in. It is used for creating fuzzy finishes and animal fur.

Fast felting and working on a core = Low gauge: #32 - #38
Fine finish, smoothing and flat wool painting = higher gauge: #38 - #42

Surfaces and Tools

Foam pads are the most popular needle felting surface. They provide a thick, firm surface to felt on and are sold in a variety of sizes. Make sure you purchase foam that has no fire retardant chemicals in it! Upolstry foam often has added fire retardant chemicals added and when the foam is repeatedly stabbed, the dust can get into your lungs. Living Felt (online) sells eco-foam with no added toxic chemicals.

Rice pads are usually made of burlap and filled with rice or grain. They are very eco-friendly. You can make your own or purchase online from Sarafina fiber arts (see resources).

Other surfaces used to felt on are wool mats and brushes. Wool mats are wet felted and tend to be thin but work well for certain smaller projects.
Brush pads are for small objects only .

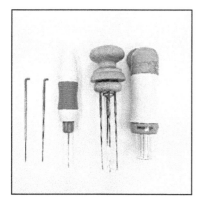

Tools that are available for needle felters include: needle holders, multi-needle holders, carders (for mixing colors) and finger guards. Sarafina fiber art also sells a large variety of inventive devices for more advanced felters to help you make fingers and toes, beaks and shapes.

Useful tools to have on hand include: pliers (for cutting wire), scissors and a measuring tape.

> WARNING
> Fire retardant chemicals are impregnated into some types of foam and can be dangerous to your health.
> Buy eco-friendly foam.

Cookie Cutter Projects

Cookie cutter projects are an important starting point in needle felting as they will develop the skills that are necessary to progress to more challenging work.

Starting with a flat object, within a boundary, will help you to understand how to make a shape and how long it takes to felt something firmly.

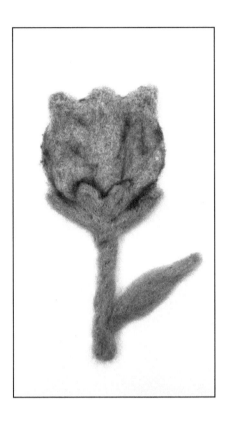

Batt is the best choice for beginners to start with. In these next few projects, we are mainly using batt. Batt felts up quickly, is easy to use and makes a firm, smooth finish. If you want to use some top for color, you can add it to the final finish.

Do not use top for the core as it would take a long time to felt firmly and you would need twice as much top as you do batt to get to the same thickness.

Cookie Cutter Tulip 2-D

Materials: Cookie cutter in a simple shape
.30 oz. of batt - your color choice

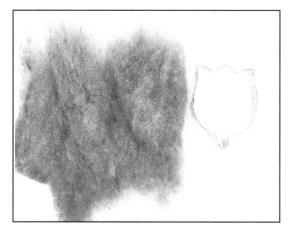

This picture shows the approximate amount of batt needed, give or take, to fill in a cookie cutter that is approximately 4" x 4".

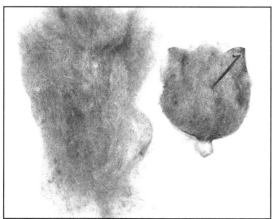

Fill the cookie cutter with half of the batt. Begin felting down. Start in the middle and work out to the edges.

When the batt in the cutter is flattened half way down, take the piece out, flip it over and then needle felt the opposite side.

Add the rest of the batt and begin the process over again.

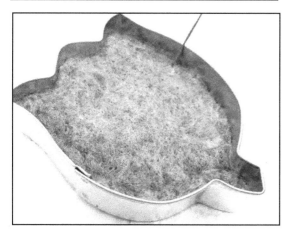

When the batt has compressed down firmly in the cutter, you should have a very firm object. Test it by squeezing. If the piece feels soft, it is not felted firmly enough. If it does not give into your touch and does not have much spring to it, then it is firm. Go around the edges with the needle to make the shape more precise.

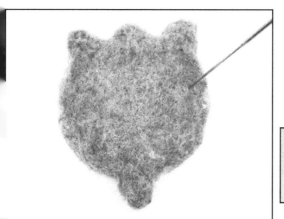

Take the piece out of the cutter and go around the entire perimeter with the needle to clean up loose wool and make the shape more specific around the edges.

> **TIP:** Be careful not to hit the needle on the edge of the metal as it will break your needle.

Gingerbread Boy

Materials: Gingerbread cookie cutter
.30 oz. of tan or brown batt
Small amounts of top in white,
red and black

This project will teach you how to make a **fine line** as well as how to make very small, **round balls.**

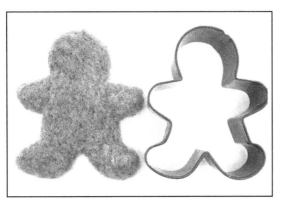

Begin making the gingerbread boy as you did the tulip. Fill the cookie cutter with tan batt and felt down. Take him out, flip him over and then fill and felt down again. Go around the edges and refine and sharpen the shape.

To make a fine line for a mouth begin twisting a very thin line of combed top. At the edge of the mouth, pin down the beginning of the twist.

Hold the other end of the twist with your fingers and felt down with another needle into the desired curved shape for a mouth.

Twisting helps tuck in all the stray wool pieces and gives you a sharper line.

For the eyes, twist a very small amount of top or batt around your needle.

Poke the needle into the eye area.

Carefully slide the twist down the needle and felt it directly onto the face with another needle.

Keep going around the edge of the eye until it is round.

The finished face.

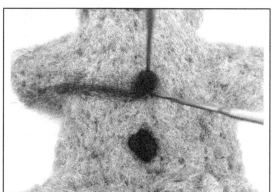

Create buttons by the same method you used to make the eyes.

Twist a thin strand of black on a needle, push down the twist to compact it into a circle shape and felt down with another needle while holding the twist/ circle in place.

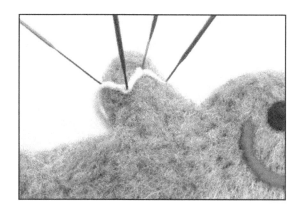

For the rick-rack trim on the arms and legs, simply twist a strand of white and pin into position. Felt down with a needle in between the the pins.

As you progress, you will be able to twist and felt as you go, without the pins.

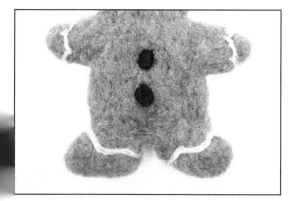

The finished body.

Rabbit

Materials: .30 oz. gray batt or roving
small amounts of batt or top: blue, white, peach/pink

This rabbit is a lesson in **how to shape a flat piece in free form**. This is a medium-soft felted project, keep this bunny a little soft so that it looks like fuzzy fur.

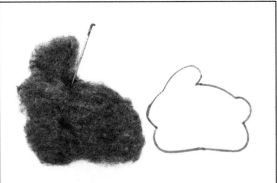

Begin by drawing an outline on paper, from a cookie cutter or an shape that you find online. Next, shape your gray batt in the form of the outline. Begin felting around the edges and the middle. Continutally hold the shape against the tracing to keep your proportions on track.

Continue to refine the rabbit by needling around the outer edges. In making this bunny, you are practicing important sculpting skills

After you are satisfied with the shape, start to add details. Put wisps of peach/pink in the ear and nose, put down a white circle for an eye and then add a black ball for the pupil (see gingerbread eyes for reference). To make a scarf, take some blue batt or top, measure the length and width you want then felt down lightly on your pad. Lift it off the pad and tie around the bunnies neck then felt down. Add a white tail (as in picture above).

Cupcake

Materials: Cookie cutter, Batt: .30 tan, light pink, dark pink
Small amounts of dark brown, white and red

Using a cupcake cutter, heart or flower - this lesson will show you how to hand blend wool to get the color you desire Your hand blending can make a new color or a striated color. Experiment and have fun with this.

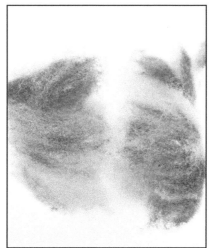

To mix two colors, layer each color on top of the other twice. Pull the layers apart with your hands and then place those two pieces on top of each other and pull again. Keep repeating this layering and pulling until you get the desired color mix. Repeating this process many times will eventually blend the colors, making a new shade.

You can also stop before the colors are completely blended, making a striated color (streaks) as in this project.

Put tan in the bottom of the cutter and put the pink-blended color on the top. Felt down firmly.

To make details, add very light layers of dark brown for the shading of the cupcake paper, a line of white, rippled across the bottom edge and a red circle on the top. Felt all this down and carefully go around the edges to sharpen details.

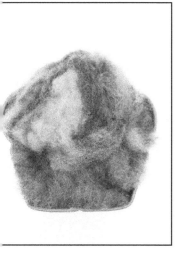

Get creative and display your projects in unique ways.

Needle felting looks great in all kinds of seasonal decor.

Needle Felting is a sustainable and eco-friendly art. Combine it with other natural materials to show off your creations.

Needle felted pieces are fun to
use as photo props.

Use your pieces in home
decor: wall hangings,
framed pictures, pillows
and wreaths.

Mr. Flat Fox

Materials: .50 oz. batt for the body: Orange or brown
Batt: .25 oz. white, black

This fox is the first lesson in free-form shaping
with attached pieces.

The fox body is a tear drop shape, mostly flat with a
slightly rounded middle stomach. Approximately
5" long.
The head is a oval 3" x 3 1/2", slightly peaked at the top.
Felt to a semi-firm feel.

Attach the head to the top of the body by overlapping
the two pieces and stabbing through both. Do this on
the top then turn the piece over and stab the other
side. Pull gently to make sure the pieces are firmly
attached.

Add a white overlay to the cheeks and body area as
shown. Felt down firmly but leave some soft edges
and a bit of puff on his stomach.

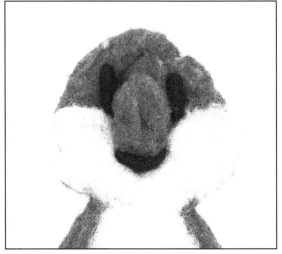

Make a nose/muzzle out of the core body batt in a rectangular shape. Felt down.

Add eyes by shaping two long, thin ovals and felt close to the nose.

The black nose is a triangle at the bottom edge.

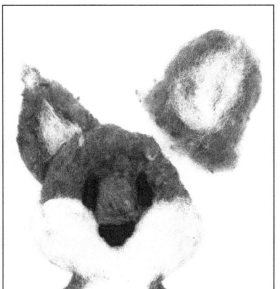

To make an ear, shape a loose triangle from the body batt and then add white to the inner area. Felt down just enough to hold the shape.

Attach to back edge of the top of the head and felt down firmly.

Continue to shape and firm the ear by needling around the outside edges.

Add white spots to the eyes and a thin black line for the mouth on the muzzle. Go around the entire project with your needle to tuck in stray wool.

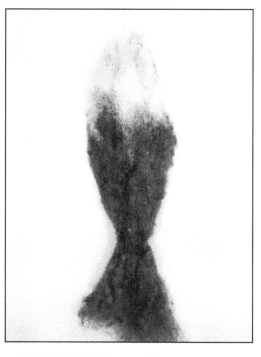

The tail is a fish shape. Shape and felt the upper part of the tail firmly and leave the bottom part of the tail unfelted.

Add white to the top of the tail.

On the back side of the fox, place the unfelted, bottom part of the tail.

Felt this firmly to the bottom half of the body, positioning the tail on an angle so it will show when viewed from the front.

For the feet, make a oval ball and slightly felt to hold the shape.
Attach this to the bottom of the body and felt firmly.
Add toes by felting down thin, black lines

TIP - All projects get slightly out of shape when you are working on them. Always do a go-round after the details are done to make the piece symmetrical.

Fluffy Bunny

Materials: Batt: .50 oz. natural, core
Batt-small amounts: peach/pink
Curly locks in color of choice
Combed top: small amounts of black and white

This bunny is a mix of 2-D and 3-D free-form sculptures. Do not felt this bunny down too flat, you want her to have a slightly puffy shape.

Start by making two square-ish ovals. Approximately 6"x 4" for the body and 4" x 3" for the head.

felt the body and the head separately and do not felt them completely flat.

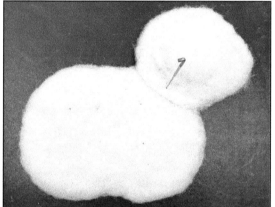

Attach the two pieces by layering one over the other close to the edges. Stab the needle through both pieces until you have a firm seam.

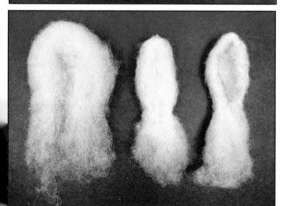

This picture shows the progression of making the ears from left to right. Fold a 2" long piece of batt in half. Begin to felt the ear by shaping around the edges and felting down in the middle.

Leave the bottom portion of the ear unfelted (for attachment to the head) and add pink to the middle ear.

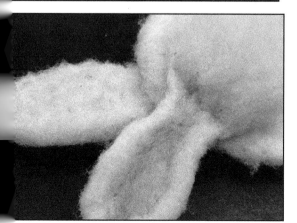

To attach the ears to the head, use the unfelted bottoms to felt onto the top of the head, placing as shown.

The back ear is placed on the back of the head, with the pink/middle facing away from the face.

For the feet, shape two ovals, one slightly larger than the other, felt lightly and then felt onto the body. The feet will become more firmly felted as you attach them to the body.

The top coat is curly-locks from the blue faced leicester breed but you can use any color of batt or top as well. This fur was for an angora-look rabbit so I kept the curls on the longer side. Loosely lay the top coat on, then lightly felt down, keeping the puffy look. Add a white tail out of the core body batt.

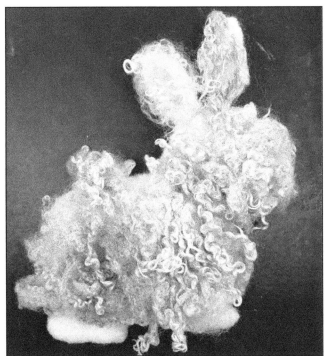

TIP: You can also make a great looking bunny without the curly locks, simply use your color of choice in batt and cover as in the picture above. Remember not to felt it down to firmly, bunnies look best with a bit of a fluff to their top coat.

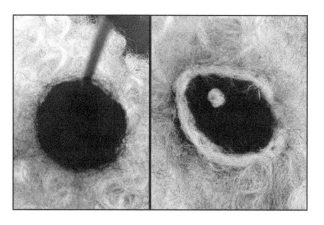

For the eye, make a circle of black and place directly onto the face and felt/shape down into an oval.

Place a thin white line (top) around the outer edge of the eye and add a small white spot to the upper edge for realism.

The nose is a small pink triangle on the muzzle. Shape as you are felting, no need to make it separately.

Needle felting can be a very zen-like experience (unless you stab yourself- don't do that). I love to felt sitting among my plants in the sunshine. Needle felting is very portable with the right kind of pad.

Snowman

Materials:
Batt: white or natural core, Batt small amouts: black and orange.
Top: black and green
Optional-sticks for arms

This snowman sculpture is a lesson in creating a 3-D stand alone sculpture. Shaping a ball is a fundamental skill that all needle felters need to master.

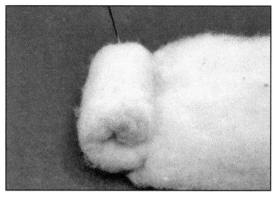

To make the balls for the snowman, begin by tightly rolling a 4" wide by 6" long piece of core batt (approx.).

For each snowball size downward, reduce the measurements by 1" for width and length.

With each roll, felt down along the edge and in the middle. Tight rolls remove the air, or loft, and makes the felting process faster. Continue rolling and felting until you have a cylinder.

Pinch the cylinder tightly and felt down to make a circular shape. Do this on the top and the bottom.

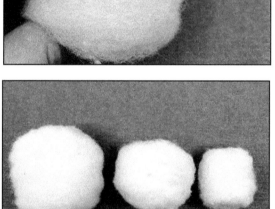

Make three balls, each one slightly smaller than the last and felt firmly.

Attach the middle ball to the bottom ball first. Push your needle through both balls at a slight angle, going around the entire ball.

Repeat with the top ball for the head.

After the pieces are attached, lay more batt on top of the snowman to cover fully and felt gently. The top cover is not felted firmly and the softness looks like snow.

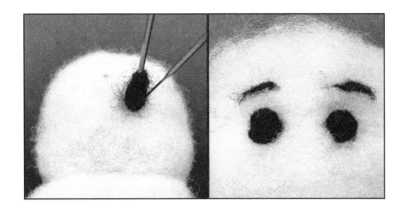

Make the eyes by wrapping black top around a needle and then sliding the wrapped wool down the needle. Push that needle deeply into the face to hold the eye while you use the other needle to compact and felt it down.

Add eyebrows with thin lines of black top.

Make two buttons in the same way you made the eyes.

The nose is made in the same way as the eye, but it is not compacted and felted down.

Wrap orange top or batt around a needle.

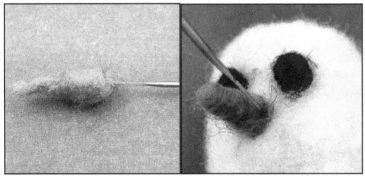

Slide the carrot nose off the needle, place the larger end onto the face and pin down with a second needle.

Carefully felt all around the base of the carrot nose and make sure it will not unravel.

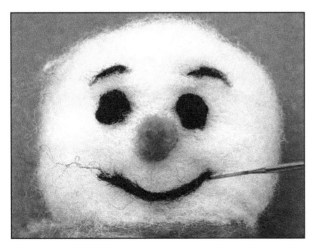

Add a mouth with a thin line of black top, starting in one corner and working towards the opposite side, tucking in stray wool threads as you go.

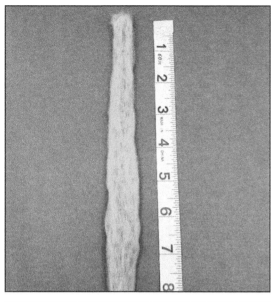

Using combed top, felt down a 2" x 8" piece.

Tie this tightly around his neck and knot. Felt down gently to hold into place.

The top hat is made out of black batt. Shape a circle and felt firmly.

Shape a cylinder and felt firmly.

Felt the bottom half of the hat directly to his head

Felt the black top cylinder directly onto the bottom half of the hat.

Go around the entire circle, making sure it is firmly felted down.

Chickadee bird

Materials:
Batt: .30 oz. natural/white and tan
Roving: brown/gray
Top: black

This project is a lesson in making a body/core out of one shape/piece.

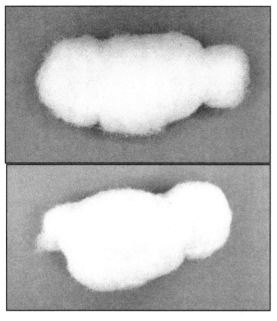

The core, body shape of this bird is made as one piece.

Start the chickadee by making a cylinder out of core batt.

Begin to shape one end of the cylinder into a round head.

Continue shaping the body by needling in a circular fashion around the parts you want to indent, as shown.

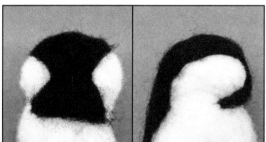

Hold the birds head to face you. Using black top, spread from under the chin to the back of the head.

Pinch the black in the middle of the face and felt down. Continue felting down all of the black area.

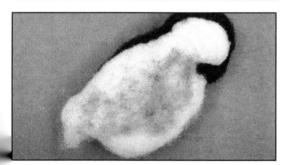

Lightly layer some light tan on the sides of the body as shown. Felt down.

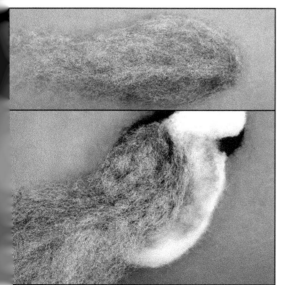

The wing is shaped out of a brown/gray roving (you can use top or batt as well).

Shape the wing loosely and then place the wing on the body.

Felt the wing in place, leaving the back part of the wing unfelted for now.

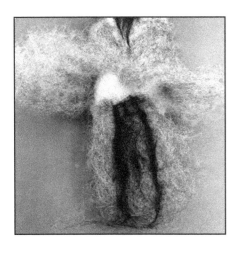

After both wings have been felted on, pull them upwards at the bottom end so you can place the tail.

The tail is a loose shaped rectangle (same roving as the wings) with thin, black lines of top.

Place this on top of the tail area and felt the tail to the body and the base. Felt the tail firmly.

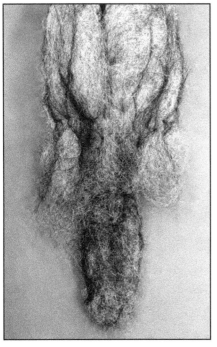

After the tail is felted, pull the feathers down and place thin, black lines (to resemble feather lines) along the length of the wings.

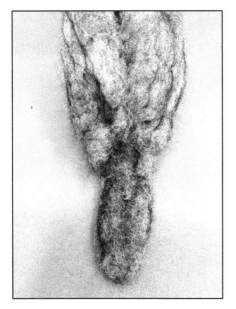

Continue felting the wings as shown. Tuck the fluffy edges under at the wing bottoms and felt down.

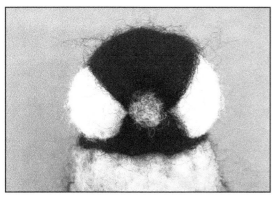

To make a beak, wind some brown/gray roving around your needle, slide down and onto the face and felt into place (refer to the snowman project/carrot nose).

Side view of bird.

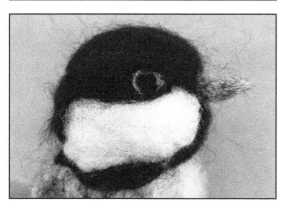

The eye is a small circle of white with a small circle of black on top of it. Place the eye inside the black top of the head area.

Felt the bird to the firmness you prefer, but try and preserve the softness of his wing feathers.

Sheep

Materials:

Batt: .50 oz. natural, core

Batt: small amounts of gray peach/pink

Top: black, white

Optional: white locks

2 Chenille stems (pipe cleaners)

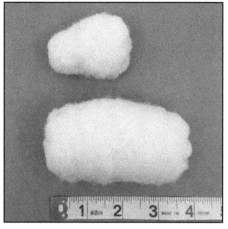

To begin the sheep make two ovals of the core batt, one larger than the other.

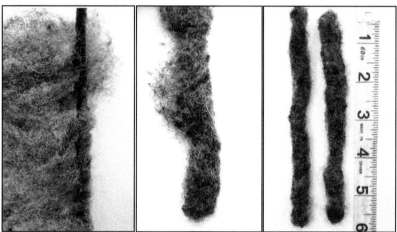

The legs are made on a chenille stems cut to 5 1/2". Begin by tightly rolling (one full turn) some gray batt onto the stem. Rip the excess batt off close to the stem, roll and felt until the leg looks well felted and it is the correct thickness in proportion to the body.

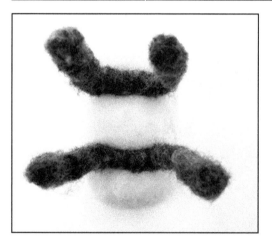

Bend the legs as shown and begin felting to the body. Try not to hit the wire stem with the needle but go along the edges. This can be challenging but it is good practice for future armature making.

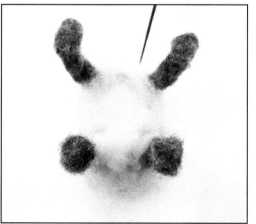

Lay some of the body batt on top of the stomach to cover the leg area. Felt down carefully. This will also help to secure the legs.

Attach the head to the body by stabbing the needle through both pieces.

Remember to push in the needle and pull out the needle at the same angle. Do not bend the needle as you are doing this as it will break.

Using gray batt, make a muzzle and cover 75% of the face.

The ears are ovals. Make the shapes but only felt 50% of the ear, leaving the bottom half open and unfelted.

Add a smidge of peach/pink to the inner ear.

Attach the ears by spreading out the unfelted batt and use that extra wool that to make an attachment.

This is a technique that makes attaching small pieces easier.

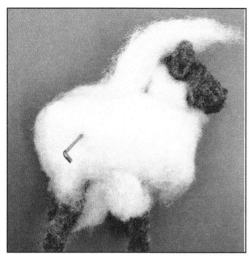

To add a top coat, spread a layer of fluffy body batt over the piece, avoiding the gray areas. You can also use locks for a curly coated sheep.

Felt the batt down but make sure to leave it a bit fluffy.

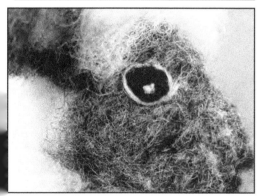

Make the eyes by shaping a small black oval onto the face with black top. Go around the eyes with thin white top (or batt) and add a bit of white to the edge of the eye for realism.

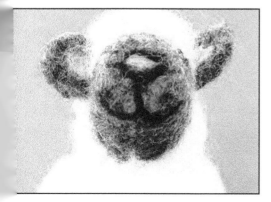

The nose is a small peach/pink triangle, outlined with a thin black line.

Bring the line down and curl off at the bottom to make the cheeks.

Add a small gray tail with an oval of batt.

The finished side view. Test the sheep's standing ability and adjust the legs as necessary. Make sure the bottom edges of the hooves are felted firmly so they don't unravel and also to give him better standing power.

This is the same sheep except the curly locks have been added on top instead of the batt top coat.

Front view of the sheep. Do your final go-round and adjust the sheep's proportions as necessary.

Storing, Organizing and Protecting Wool

Storing wool can be a challenge. It doesn't weigh much but its loft can make it hard to compress and store.

The first consideration in wool storage needs to be protecting it from pets, moths (bugs) and mildew. Using a closed system is usually the best way to protect wool

Closed wool storage ideas: Plastic bins, plastic bags, and glass jars. Hanging shoe organizers work well if there is no pets or insects around (it is an open system). Open systems also include wall shelving or bins. If you leave your wool in open storage, make sure you don't have a bug/pest problem in your area. Basements can be moldy and wool can pick up an mildew scent to it if it's stored near high humidity areas. Essential oils or cedar wood balls can help repel bugs. Never use moth balls as this will give the wool a very bad odor.

Wool can be organized by: color, product type (batt, roving, locks, etc...) or breed. By far the most popular way to organize is by color.

If you do get bugs in your wool, you will notice tiny black specks, worm-like creatures or moths. If you suspect them, you can try freezing your wool. Bag it up and put it in the freezer for a few weeks. Take it out and see if any bugs still hatch. Keep isolated for another month.

Wool is a real danger to pets, they can ingest it and it can get stuck in their digestive track so make sure your storage system is pet proof.

Koala Bear

Materials:

Batt: .50 gray

Small amounts of batt: black, white, pink/peach

Top: small amount of white

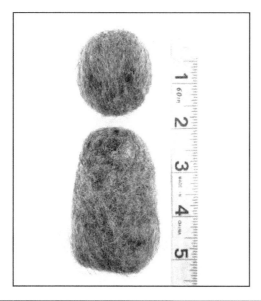

For the Koala body, make a cylinder/oval shape, approximately 3 1/2 " long by 2" wide . Flatten the bottom end (so he can sit properly).

For the head, make a circle, approx. 1 1/2".

Felt to a medium firm feel.

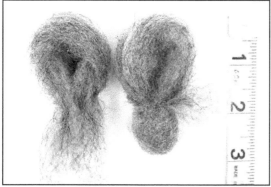

The legs (and the arms) are 4" long pieces of roving or batt, folded over.

Pinch at about 1 1/2 " and felt.

Fold the unfelted, bottom piece upward, felt lightly. This will form the foot.

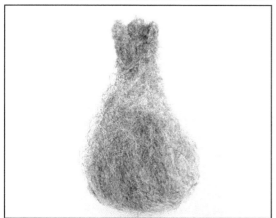

Leave the top portion of the leg unfelted and felt down the foot.

After the foot area is flattened, take your needle and create toes by pushing into the wool and indenting to make three equal size toes.

Take the leg and felt directly onto the body. This will flatten the haunch/leg area and secure it to the body.

Create the arms in the same way you made the legs but add 1/2" an inch to the length.

Make the top part of the arm thinner than the leg haunch.

Felt the arms onto the body.

Felt the head onto the body by plunging the needle between the two pieces. Go around the entire head.

After the head is secure, add a small amount of the body batt to wrap around the neck and felt this down. This creates a neck for the koala.

Lay a thin layer of white on the koalas belly and up towards his chin

 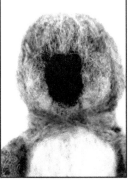

For the muzzle, add a small piece of body batt to the front of the face, from the forehead to the nose. This will help his face protrude outward for a koala-like profile

For the nose, shape a rectangle and soften the edges, place onto the face/muzzle and felt down tightly.

Add peach to the nose for nostrils.

For the chin, make a thin line of black top to outline the area as shown.

Make an eye by shaping an oval and felting onto the eye area. Outline with a thin, white line of top and add a tiny white spot to the inner eye edge.

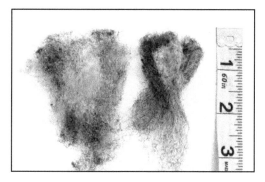

Shape the ears by folding the batt over and forming a loose triangle. Add white and then a bit of peach to the inner part. This picture shows the initial shaping (left) and then the first felting (right). Leave the bottom end of the ear unfelted for attachment purposes.

Open the bottom ear fluff and spread evenly on both sides as you place it on the side on the head. Using the unfelted wool, attach to the head and felt the ear at the bottom. Don't felt down all the fluff but instead fold some backwards so it forms the furry edge of the ear.

When you are working on a realistic looking animal, always research and study pictures of the real thing first and refer to those pictures throughout the making of your project. This gives you an understanding of the animal from different angles and helps you get the proportions correct.

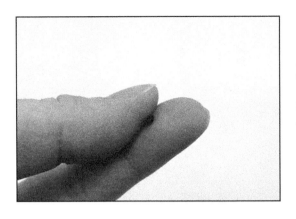

For the claws, roll a very tiny amount of wool between your fingers to form into balls/cylinders, 12 in total. Small amounts of wool can actually felt together by this method.

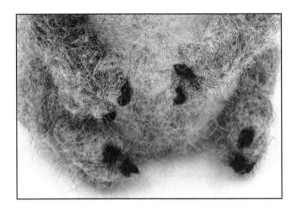

Carefully attach the claws to the ends of the toes and feet and felt down. This is delicate work and takes time.

For the final felt, you can use a #40 needle to felt down the fuzzies, or you can leave the fuzzy look for a more furry appearance.

For new and FREE projects and tutorials like this one, go to www.naturecrafty.com and sign up for monthly newsletters.

Landscape picture
2 - Dimensional Wool Painting

Materials:

Fabric: wool, felt or burlap 8" x 10"

Batt: dark purple and light lavender

Top: light green

Locks: white

Cut an 8" x 10" piece of fabric out, stretch it across a foam pad and pin the edges to hold it.

Using a template, trace the heart by making **pencil dots** (represented by the purple circles). It's easier to cover dots with wool than it is a solid line.

Start laying the batt down in the hearts. Use a #38 needle to go around the edges and then use a multi-needle tool (if you have one) filled with #40 or #42 needles to flatten down the inner part.

Using a multi tool with fine needles cuts down felting time.

This is the view before the inner heart is felted down. Make sure your edges are clean before felting down the middle.

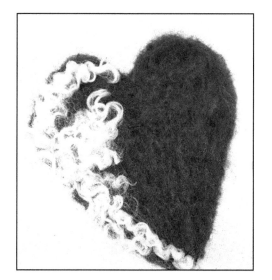

You can add curly locks for textural and visual interest if desired. Felt down lightly to leave a spring in the curl.

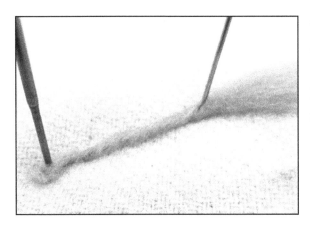

To make the lavender stems, take some thin strands of light green top and felt one edge into the fabric.

Next, twist the wool with your fingers and begin felting it down as you twist.

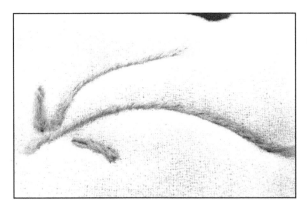

Add another stem and two leaves. Make sure your twists are felted down tightly.

For the flowers, take a small bit of each of the colors of the hearts and twist together, felting the edge nearest to the stem.

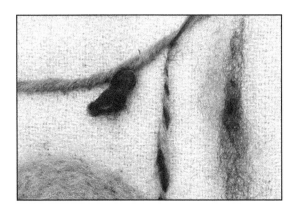

When the wool is securely felted to the stem, continue twisting until it doubles back onto itself and then felt firmly to the fabric.

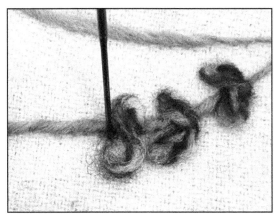

To make symetrical flower buds, use the same technique as above but use more wool so your twist can also extend to the other side.

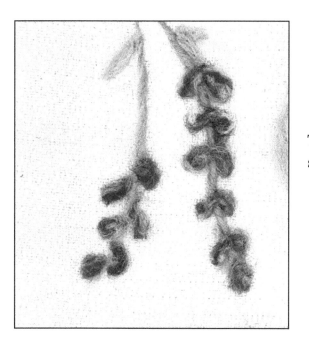

These two stems show single buds as well as symetrical buds.

This piece can be framed, sewn onto a pillow or made into a small wall hanging.

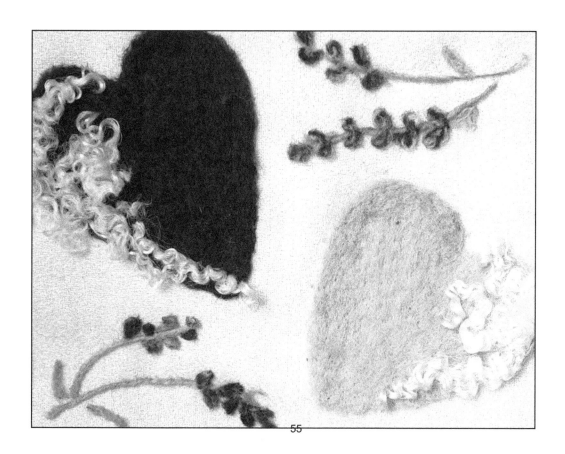

Resources

USA

Sarafina Fiber Art
www.sarafinafiberart.com
Fabulous selection of wool, tools and kits

Living Felt
www.livingfelt.com
Large variety of wool (needle and wet) and
eco friendly foam

The Woolery
www.woolery.com
Fiber for all branches of the fiber arts
community

Canada

Fibercraft
www.fibrecraft.ca
Impressive array of fibers and supplies

UK and EU

The Makerss
www.themakerss.co.uk
Extensive needle felting wool and supplies

Sweet Pea Dolls
www.sweetpeadolls.co.uk
Inspiring range of fibers, tools and kits.
Alternative fibers

World of Wool
www.worldofwool.co.uk
Huge variety of wool and tools and delivers
worldwide

The Dyeing House Gallery Shop - Italy
A vast assortment of high quality wool and
unusual colors

The Wollknoll Shop - Germany
www.wollknoll.eu/shop/

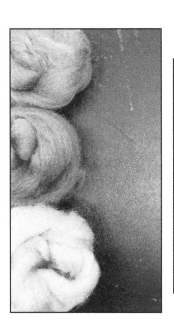

More ways to source wool:

Join a local fiber group in your area, they have good
information on local farms and small producers.

Etsy can also be a good source for quality wool products
(but always check reviews!).

Try to attend Fiber Festivals in your area as that is one of
the most exciting ways to stock up on wool. Chatting with
vendors is a great way to learn about local wool sources.

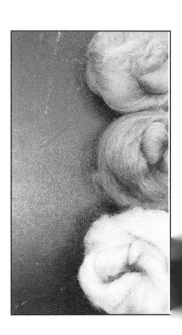

Ounces / Pounds	Grams	Ounces / Pounds	Grams
1oz	28g	16oz = 1lb	454g
2oz	57g	1.5lb	680g
3oz	85g	2lb	907g
4oz = 0.25 lb	113g	2.5lb	1134g
5oz	142g	3lb	1361g
6oz	170g	3.5lb	1588g
7oz	198g	4lb	1814g
8oz = 0.5lb	227g	4.5lb	2041g
9oz	255g	5lb	2268g
10oz	283g		
11oz	312g	Wool amounts given in the
12oz - 0.75lb	340g	materials section are approximate.
13oz	369g	You may need a bit more or less
14oz	397g	depending the size of your piece.
15oz	425g	

Lori Rea is an Amazon ranked, best selling author in the arts and crafts genre. A spirited advocate of nature crafting and a self taught needle felter, Lori picked up her first needle and began stabbing wool in 2010. This new passion quickly spiraled into an over abundance of creatures, a tutorial website: Naturecrafty, and her first book, "Needle felting for Beginners". A floral designer by trade, with an eye for design, Lori's projects have garnered praise for being beautiful and intricate yet simple to create.

Stay In Touch!
I give my readers loads of freebies and the chance to download new books for free!
Sign up:
www.naturecrafty.com

Facebook
Nature Crafts

Instagram
@naturecrafter

Needle Felting
A Complete Course

The next book in the Needle Felting Series!

From Beginner to Advanced
with Step-by-Step Instructions

Lori Rea

Needle Felting - A Complete Course
* 14 project lessons
* Basic techniques glossary
* 3-D and 2-D projects
* Armature making
* Comprehensive guide to needles, wool and tools
* Tips and Hacks
* Resources
* Inspiring artists share their advice and photos

Projects from
"Needle Felting - A Complete Course"
On Amazon now!

Join the herd and be a part of the needle felting community! We are waiting for ewe!

For Felting Inspiration

Join online Facebook groups:

Needle Felting
UK Needle Felting
Sarafina
Living Felt

CPSIA information can be obtained
at www.ICGtesting.com
Printed in the USA
LVHW070605230322
714081LV00007B/362